LIFE IN A GRASSLAND

LIFE IN A GRASSLAND

DOROTHY HINSHAW PATENT
PHOTOGRAPHS BY WILLIAM MUÑOZ

Lerner Publications Company
Minneapolis

For all those who passed before us
—D. H. P. and W. M.

Text copyright © 2003 by Dorothy Hinshaw Patent
Photographs copyright © 2003 by William Muñoz, except where noted

Lerner Publications Company
A division of Lerner Publishing Group
241 First Avenue North
Minneapolis, MN 55401 U.S.A.

Website address: www.lernerbooks.com

Library of Congress Cataloging-in-Publication Data

Patent, Dorothy Hinshaw.
  Life in a grassland / by Dorothy Hinshaw Patent ; photos by William Muñoz.
     p.   cm. — (Ecosystems in action)
  Summary: Examines the physical features, processes, and many different species of
plants and animals that make up the ecosystem of the American tallgrass prairie.
   ISBN: 0–8225–2139–3 (lib. bdg. : alk. paper)
    1. Grassland ecology—Juvenile literature. [1. Grasslands. 2. Grassland ecology.
3. Ecology.] I. Muñoz, William, ill. II. Title. III. Series.
QH541.5.P7 P38 2003
577.4—dc21   2002000952

Manufactured in the United States of America
1 2 3 4 5 6 – JR – 08 07 06 05 04 03

CONTENTS

WHAT IS AN ECOSYSTEM?

An ecosystem is a particular community of living things interacting with each other and their environment. Just about everything is involved in an ecosystem—the weather, the soil, the air, the plants, the animals, and all the other living things, such as bacteria and fungi.

The tallgrass prairie ecosystem is very different from other ecosystems, such as an old growth forest or a sagebrush desert. While there may be areas where two ecosystems intermingle along their edges, each ecosystem is easy to recognize. The tallgrass prairie merges into forests to the east and the mixed prairie to the west. While the tallgrass and mixed prairies are both grasslands and share many kinds of animals and plants, each is home to species unique to its ecosystem. The plains pocket gopher and Franklin's ground squirrel both live in the tallgrass prairie but rarely in the mixed prairie. On the other hand, the swift fox and the mule deer inhabit the mixed prairie but not the tallgrass.

An ecosystem's physical traits, such as soil type, climate, and weather patterns, as well as the plants and animals that live there, define the ecosystem. The amount of rainfall, for example, is very important in making an ecosystem what it is. Precipitation such as rain or snow falls at least

> **GRASSES GROW IN MANY DIFFERENT ECOSYSTEMS, BUT THEY DOMINATE OTHER PLANT SPECIES ONLY IN THE VARIOUS GRASSLAND ECOSYSTEMS.**

sometime during each year everywhere on the earth, except in the very driest of deserts. Rainfall on the tallgrass prairie is greater than on the short-grass prairie. The more abundant rain allows taller grasses to grow. But the tallgrass prairie has less rain than an eastern forest. That's one reason few trees grow on the prairie, except near bodies of water like ponds and streams.

Some elements are unique to a particular ecosystem, but others are shared with other ecosystems. For example, the black-tailed prairie dog lives in mixed and short-grass prairies but not in tallgrass prairie. Other animals, like the American kestrel, are much more widely adapted and can be found in ecosystems all over the United States and much of Canada. Grasses grow in many different ecosystems, but they dominate other plant species only in the various grassland ecosystems.

HOW AN ECOSYSTEM WORKS

Chemicals such as water, nitrogen, and carbon move from one part of an ecosystem to another. Energy also flows throughout all ecosystems. The energy of the sun, which reaches the earth as sunshine, is transferred through the ecosystem. The chemical reactions of life, called metabolism, require the input of energy. Without plants to capture the sun's energy, most of the earth's ecosystems would run out of energy and die.

The sun's energy is stored in the leaves, stems, roots, and flowers of the plants. As prairie grasses take in the energy of the sun, the grasses grow taller and their

clumps become thicker. This is called primary production, the first capturing of energy and turning it into living material.

Next, a grazing animal, like a grasshopper, eats the grass. The grasshopper and other animals that eat plants are called primary consumers. Some of the sun's energy captured by the plant is converted into the growing body of the grasshopper.

The plant eaters need to watch out for predators, the animals that eat other animals. A predator, like a small snake, eats the grasshopper. The snake in turn is captured by a hawk. The chemicals and energy of the grasshopper are transferred to the snake, then to the hawk. Both the snake and the hawk, which eat other animals, are called secondary consumers.

When the hawk dies, its body is consumed by worms, maggots, fungi, and bacteria. These living things that break down dead matter are called decomposers. What is left returns to the soil to nourish new plants. This constant recycling of energy and chemicals helps keep an ecosystem running smoothly.

Ecologists are also interested in the input and the output of an ecosystem, the things that enter or leave it. Besides the sunlight that feeds plants, a red-tailed hawk that moves to the prairie from the nearby forest is part of the input. Rainfall that soaks the ground and drains into a river that flows toward the sea is part of the output.

The most important thing about looking at an ecosystem is seeing how everything that happens affects the system as a whole. In a healthy ecosystem, recycling keeps materials available for the next round of production. The input of energy and materials must be sufficient to fuel production. Different species of plants and animals live in different grasslands. But all grassland ecosystems rely on grasses as the main primary producers. The energy is first taken in by grasses, and the grasses sustain all prairie life.

ORIGINAL RANGE OF GRASSLANDS IN NORTH AMERICA

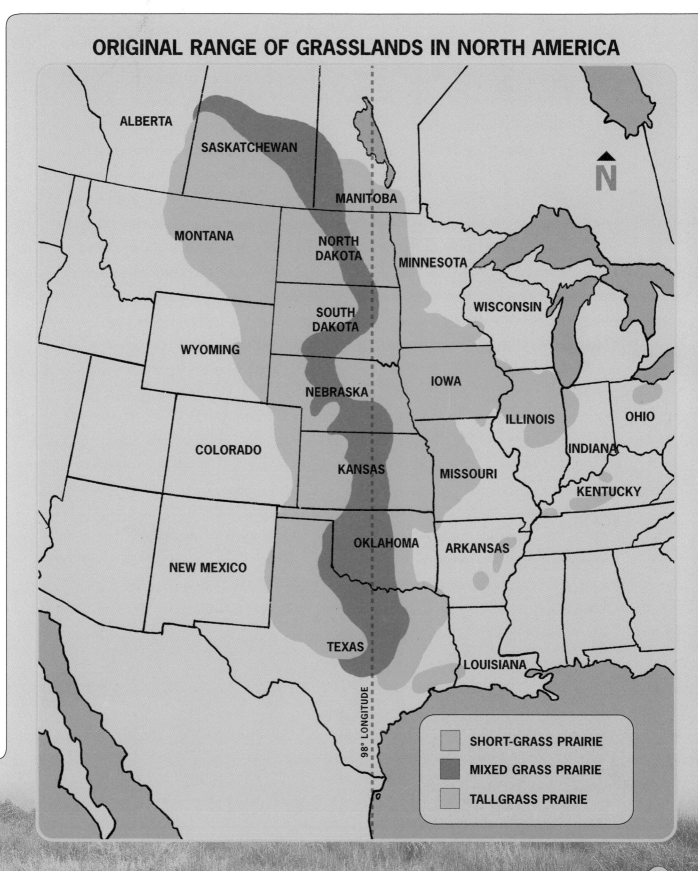

ALBERTA

SASKATCHEWAN

MANITOBA

MONTANA

NORTH DAKOTA

MINNESOTA

WISCONSIN

SOUTH DAKOTA

WYOMING

IOWA

NEBRASKA

ILLINOIS

OHIO

INDIANA

COLORADO

KANSAS

MISSOURI

KENTUCKY

NEW MEXICO

OKLAHOMA

ARKANSAS

TEXAS

LOUISIANA

98° LONGITUDE

N

SHORT-GRASS PRAIRIE

MIXED GRASS PRAIRIE

TALLGRASS PRAIRIE

CHAPTER 1

A WORLD OF GRASS AND SUN

Mile after mile of green and gold grasslands used to stretch across parts of every continent on the earth except Antarctica. Perhaps a quarter of the earth's surface was cloaked in grasslands. Grasslands take on different names around the world—steppes in Eurasia, pampas in South America, rangelands in Australia, savannas in Africa, and prairies in North America.

Almost a third of central North America was once made up of grasslands. The prairies swept across the center of the continent, from near the Rocky Mountains in the west to the edges of the eastern forests, and from the plains of Canada southward deep into Texas.

Grasslands are areas where various kinds of grass are the most abundant plants and where few or no trees grow.

THE TALLGRASS PRAIRIE IN SPRINGTIME

Of all the different kinds of flowering plants around the world, grasses form the fourth largest family after the daisy, orchid, and pea families.

All kinds of grasslands share two important features, grass and plenty of sunlight, but they also have their differences. The North American prairies consist of three types of prairie—the short-grass prairie toward the Rocky Mountains, the tallgrass prairie across the east, and the mixed prairie in between. Each of these types of prairie forms its own ecosystem.

The western short-grass prairie is made up largely of grasses about 20 inches (0.5 meters) tall. Prairie dog towns provide homes for many animals. The cool burrows, when abandoned by the prairie dogs, also shelter prairie rattlesnakes, burrowing owls, and black-footed ferrets.

In the band of mixed prairie that runs through North America from Texas to Saskatchewan, the grasses generally stand from 2 to 4 feet (about 1 meter) tall. Buffalo, more properly called bison, once thrived on the mixed prairie. Hundreds of thousands of these powerful animals grazed their way across the prairie.

The western edge of the tallgrass prairie ecosystem runs roughly along the 98th meridian of longitude. It's hard to say just where the tallgrass prairie area begins and ends, especially to the east, as there are patches of tallgrass mixed in with forest in several states. The tallgrass prairie is a dramatic landscape rich with life. The graceful grasses typically reach 5 to 6 feet (nearly 2 meters) tall. In some areas, they can grow to 12 feet (3.7 meters). When the wind blows across the

(ABOVE) **BLACK-FOOTED FERRET *(MUSTELA NIGRIPES)***

(LEFT) **BLACK-TAILED PRAIRIE DOG *(CYNOMYS LUDOVICIANUS)***

tallgrass prairie, it looks as if waves are rolling gently over the surface of a great green ocean with no shoreline in sight.

ORIGIN OF THE PRAIRIE

The forces that created the prairie acted long ago. The geology of North America between the Rocky Mountains and the Appalachian Mountains is very stable. Unlike much of the earth's crust, this region has stayed in the same place for about five hundred million years. During this time, the Appalachians and later the Rockies were created when moving pieces of the earth's crust smashed up against one another, pushing land up toward the sky.

When the Rockies were created about sixty-five million years ago, they forever changed conditions on the plains to their east. Prevailing winds blowing from west to east have carried eroded soil from the mountains out onto the plains ever since. Over the eons, different kinds of soil-forming minerals have been blown over the plains. Fine-textured soil ended up along the Missouri and Mississippi Rivers. Sandy material was deposited as large sand dunes in southwestern Nebraska.

The closer the land to the Rockies, the more sediment has been deposited there. Over time, the differences in the amount of deposits led to a gradual rise in altitude from close to sea level at the western edge of the Appalachians to more than 1 mile (0.6 kilometers) high just east of the Rockies.

The Rocky Mountains have another important effect on the

THIS ADDED MOISTURE MEANS THAT MORE RAIN FALLS ON THE EASTERN PART OF THE PRAIRIE, ALLOWING THE TALL GRASSES TO GROW.

plains—the weather. When clouds encounter mountains, they tend to release their moisture as rain or snow. By the time clouds pass over the Rockies, most of the moisture is gone, and little rain or snow falls. As the air flows eastward across the Great Plains, it joins with very moist air moving northward from the Gulf of Mexico. This added moisture means that more rain falls on the eastern part of the prairie, allowing the tall grasses to grow.

Glaciers also helped shape the plains. From two million to ten thousand years ago, during four major glacial periods, different parts of the plains were covered with sheets of ice up to 1 mile (0.6 kilometers) thick. These masses of ice carved and shaped the land beneath them. They scraped up rock in one area and deposited it in another. Piles of glacial gravel became hills or ridges. Huge blocks of ice left by glaciers pressed down on the earth, creating the ponds and lakes that dot the plains.

THE TALLGRASS CLIMATE

The tallgrass prairie receives from 25 to 39 inches (63 to 99 centimeters) of rain

THE ROCKY MOUNTAINS MEET THE GRASSLANDS.

during the year. The timing of the rain is vitally important. Half the rain usually falls from May through July, when it is most needed by growing plants.

Summer is hot and humid throughout the tallgrass prairie. The plains, including the tallgrass prairie, are an area of often-violent summer weather. With no mountains to block them, cold, dry air masses from the north and warm, moist air masses from the Gulf of Mexico both flow over the plains. When a cold front from the north meets warm, moist air from the south, hailstorms and tornadoes can form.

Winter on the tallgrass varies a great deal from south to north. At the southern end, in Oklahoma, a typical January means high temperatures around 46° Fahrenheit (8° Celsius) and lows of about 27° Fahrenheit (−3° Celsius). In the far northern tallgrass prairie, in Canada, a typical January high is only 7° Fahrenheit (−14° Celsius), while lows are about

(ABOVE) **AN EARLY SUMMER STORM MOVES OVER THE TALLGRASS PRAIRIE.**

(RIGHT) **FIRE HELPS MAINTAIN THE PRAIRIE BY KILLING TREE SEEDLINGS.**

−13° Fahrenheit (−25° Celsius). While Oklahoma can get as cold as −2° Fahrenheit (−19° Celsius), the temperature on the Canadian prairie can plummet to −48° Fahrenheit (−44° Celsius).

MAINTAINING THE PRAIRIE

Several wet years in a row can allow tree seedlings to take hold, turning the tallgrass prairie into a forest. Once trees become established, their roots can grow deep enough to get sufficient water even in a dry year. Even so, the tallgrass prairie has managed to survive for thousands of years.

First of all, the dense mat of grasses makes it difficult for a tree seed to reach the ground, where it could sprout. When a tree seed does manage to sprout, the little seedling has to struggle its way through the stems and leaves of the grass before it can reach the sun. Even if it grows tall, the young tree faces other threats. The wind blows hard and often on the prairie, which makes life difficult for trees. Wind breaks tree branches, and it drives dust and sand before it, which can damage tender leaves.

The biggest enemy of trees on the prairie is fire. The prairie is a land of lightning and thunder, and dry grass burns easily. All it takes to set the prairie ablaze is a bolt of lightning striking the dry ground. The wind does the rest, fanning the flames and carrying the fire far across the land. Even if a seedling manages to survive and begins to grow sturdy branches above the grass, it has little chance of growing tall enough and with thick enough bark to survive a fire before one comes along.

Trees carry their future points of growth, called buds, aboveground. There they can be killed by fire.

While fire destroys young trees, it doesn't kill the other prairie plants. During the spring and fall, when dead, dry grasses can fuel a hot fire, the buds of prairie plants are at or just below ground level. The energy for future growth is stored in the roots below the ground. The dead grasses burn hot. At 3 feet (1 meter) above the ground, they can reach 400° Fahrenheit (about 200° Celsius). But below the soil surface, where the roots and buds are, the temperature only increases a few degrees.

Large animals, such as bison, can easily outrun a fire. Birds merely need to fly. Snakes, lizards, and toads find shelter in the burrows of moles, ground squirrels, and badgers. Certainly, some small mammals and many insects and spiders perish in the fires. But before long, as the grasses grow fresh and tender, new individuals of these species soon make homes there again.

Grass takes two to three years to decompose, but fire releases the nutrients in dead grass stems and leaves instantly, making the nutrients available for the next generation of shoots. Fire also removes the thick layer of dead plants on the soil surface, so the new shoots don't have to struggle through layers of dead material to reach the sun. The exposed soil surface can soak up rain more easily, and the black color of the charred plants absorbs heat from the sun, speeding spring growth. The burned, blackened ground can be 10° Fahrenheit (6° Celsius) warmer than unburned prairie in May or June.

CAPTURING ENERGY

Almost all ecosystems on the earth are fueled by energy from the sun, and plants are the organisms with the equipment to capture that energy. Have you ever wondered why plants are green when they are growing? That green color comes from a complicated chemical called chlorophyll in the plants' cells. Chlorophyll soaks up the sun's energy. The plant cells then convert the energy into chemical energy through a set of chemical reactions called photosynthesis. First the energy is trapped in special energy-rich molecules. Then that energy is used to combine water and carbon dioxide to make molecules of sugar. The chemical energy in the sugar is the energy source for all the plant's activities. The energy can be stored as sugar or other carbohydrates such as starch, or it can be used to fuel the plant's growth.

Photosynthesis does more than capture sunlight into a form that can be used by living things. Oxygen is also released during photosynthesis. Most living things need oxygen to fuel their own energy-producing chemical reactions. Some bacteria and a few other life-forms can live without oxygen and have ways of obtaining energy other than through photosynthesis. But without this amazing process, there would be little life on the earth beyond microscopic, single-celled organisms.

PRAIRIE PLANTS

Grasses define the prairie. Grasses are very successful, especially in harsh climates. They can endure drying wind,

PHOTOSYNTHESIS PROVIDES THE ENERGY FOR THE GROWTH OF PRAIRIE GRASSES.

drought, and bitterly cold winters better than most plants. They survive because their roots penetrate deep within the soil, sometimes twice as far as their leaves stretch upward toward the sun. This helps them to find moisture even when the surface of the ground is dry. Grasses also survive because their leaves are long and slender, with little surface area for losing moisture. When it gets really dry, the leaves of many prairie grasses curl around into long tubes, further lessening water loss. Grass bends in the wind, but it pops right back up again when the breezes fade. As grass matures, a tough chemical called silicon dioxide is deposited in the outer layer of the stems, strengthening them against the wind.

Plants called forbs dot the prairie. Forbs are herbaceous plants, meaning that they don't have woody stems. Forbs have leaves that are relatively wide compared to those of grasses. The wildflowers that can make a prairie glow

(ABOVE) **A BUMBLEBEE *(BOMBUS)* GATHERS POLLEN AND NECTAR FROM A PURPLE CONEFLOWER *(ECHINACEA PURPUREA)*.**

(RIGHT) **POLLEN GRAINS HANG FROM GRASS FLOWERS.**

with color are forbs. The bright colors and delightful scents of flowers attract animals called pollinators. Pollinators, such as bees and butterflies, carry a material called pollen from one flower to another. The pollen, which is usually yellow, contains the male reproductive cells of the plant. A pollinator, such as a bee, visits a flower to collect a sweet liquid called nectar. As the bee enters the flower, its body becomes dusted with pollen. At the next flower, some of the pollen gets brushed off the bee onto a structure of the flower called the stigma. The stigma is at the end of a stalk called the style. The pollen sends a microscopic tube down through the style. Then a male nucleus travels through the tube to the ovary of the flower, where it combines with a female nucleus. This is the beginning of a seed.

Some forbs are annuals, meaning the plants live only one year. The seeds of annuals survive through the winter at the surface of the ground. They sprout and grow quickly into new plants in the moist spring. Then they bloom before the prairie dries out, forming new seeds that will sprout and grow the following year.

Other forbs are biennials. They live for two years. The first year, biennials put all their energy into growing big and strong. They store the energy they have collected in their roots and in a small cluster of leaves that hugs the ground during the winter. During their second year, biennials produce flowers as well as new leaves. After seeds form, the biennials die.

Perennials are plants that live for a number of years. Some perennials live for decades, while others survive for only a few years. Most perennials have long roots that push deeply into the soil. Their leaves tend to be tough and leathery, which protects them from drying out and from being completely eaten by grazing animals.

Trees, shrubs, and bushes are all woody plants. Very few woody plants live in the prairie. Where water comes close to the surface, a patch of wild roses or perhaps some wild fruit might grow, but that is rare.

Trees are also very rare out on the prairie. But an occasional bur oak manages to put down roots among the grasses. These trees are adapted to survive out in the hot, dry sun. When a bur oak seed sprouts, it sends down a long taproot to gather moisture. The taproot can grow 4 feet (over 1 meter) long its first year. As the young tree grows upward, it produces wide branches that shade the ground, helping to keep the ground in which its roots grow from drying out. The leaves of a bur oak are leathery, reducing water loss. Its corky bark helps protect the trunk from the frequent prairie fires.

The shores of rivers, streams, and ponds furnish perfect habitat for bushes and trees that can't get enough water to survive out on the prairie itself. Most prairie trees are found there. Cottonwood trees need lots of moisture and are common along prairie waterways. Elm, ash, and box elder grow there, too, as well as pussy willows and wild roses.

ANIMALS OF THE PRAIRIE

Grasses and forbs provide anchoring points for spiders to build their webs and hiding places for insects among their leaves and stems. On the ground between the clumps of grass, mice and other small animals move from place to place. A grassland also makes a perfect home for snakes. A snake can wend its way through even the most densely growing grasses. It's easy for a snake to hide in the tall grass both from its prey and from predators that might eat it.

Half a dozen kinds of mice live in the tall grass, making tunnels between the plants on the surface. Moles, gophers, and badgers burrow in the ground. Weasels hunt the mice and other small animals, while skunks trudge along, feeding on everything from grasshoppers to mice to small birds and their eggs.

Although the grasses are more common on the prairie, the forbs also provide animals with anchoring points and hiding places. Forbs have leaves that caterpillars can eat and flowers that nourish bees and butterflies.

Waterways are important to prairies, too. Frogs and painted turtles inhabit ponds and streams. Birds such as cranes, ducks, and geese stop to feed in ponds and streams as they migrate. Some of these birds also raise their families along the prairie waterways. Prairie ponds and streams are home to a great variety of insects and fish.

The trees and bushes that grow on shore provide vital places for many prairie birds to nest. The trees shade the ground and the water, so there are cool places for animals to rest.

Coyotes and foxes stalk the tallgrass prairie in search of mice, rabbits, and other prey, including nestlings of birds that nest on the ground, such as grouse and meadowlarks. Birds are the most obvious prairie animals. Since they can fly from place to place so easily, most birds found in the tallgrass prairie are also found in other kinds of grasslands. Birds familiar almost anywhere in the lower forty-eight states, such as turkey vultures, mourning doves, and red-tailed hawks, are as much at home on the prairie as at the edge of a forest. Some birds, however, such as the sharp-tailed grouse, live only in mixed and tallgrass prairie.

THROUGH THE YEAR

Intense sunlight radiates energy onto the prairie, giving the plants plenty of energy

WESTERN BOX TURTLE (TERRAPENE ORNATA)

MEADOWLARKS (STURNELLA) THRIVE ON THE PRAIRIE.

for production. With little shade to interrupt this flow of energy, prairie grasses can grow very fast. During the summer, when the grasses and forbs are growing, providing food for primary consumers, the prairie teems with life. Grasshoppers and bison alike graze on the nutritious young leaves, recycling plant material into animal substance.

Life comes and goes rapidly on the prairie. Lightning fires burn the dead grass, recycling minerals to nourish new growth. Insects hatch and die every day, allowing a rapid turnover of energy. Meanwhile, the roots of grasses and forbs store up energy in the form of carbohydrates to help them grow again after fire, drought, and winter.

At the end of summer, most prairie birds form large flocks and leave for the south, creating output of energy into other ecosystems until the next spring, when the sun's warmth will once again turn the prairie into an intensely productive land.

CHAPTER 2
AMONG THE GRASSES

If you look out over the tallgrass prairie, especially in late spring or early summer, you'll see all sorts of plants that look different from one another. The grasses themselves come in a variety of heights, colors, and types of seed heads. About 150 different species, or kinds, of grasses grow in the tallgrass prairie. The lovely prairie wildflowers bloom in rainbow shades of yellow, red, purple, blue, and white.

Perennial grasses are by far the most abundant producers of the prairie. The various species are adapted to different growing conditions. You may think of prairies as being flat, but they aren't flat at all. Some prairies have gentle swells and dips, while others have taller hills. The tallest grasses grow in the lower areas, where water drains from the rises and hills. Species that need less water grow on the

MANY WILDFLOWERS, SUCH AS BLACK-EYED SUSANS (*RUDBECKIA HIRTA*), GROW IN THE TALLGRASS PRAIRIE.

slopes, while those that can survive much drier conditions live along the crests of the swells and on top of the hills.

The vast majority of prairie plants belong to just four groups: cool season grasses; warm season grasses; members of the daisy family; and members of the pea family, also called legumes. The daisy and most of the pea family plants are forbs.

The cool season grasses, such as Kentucky bluegrass, take advantage of the wet weather in the spring. They have already produced seeds by late spring or early summer. During the hot months, they stop growing and rest. Then, when cool weather comes again in the fall, they grow once more. The cool season grasses are more common the farther north the prairie stretches.

Most tallgrass prairie species are warm season grasses that don't start growing until later in the spring. Once they start, warm season grasses grow all summer. They produce their seeds in late summer or early fall. Warm season species are adapted to the hot, dry summer and thrive after the earlier grasses have faded. Their stems have a tough outer layer that helps prevent drying, and their roots are deep.

THE VAST MAJORITY OF PRAIRIE PLANTS BELONG TO JUST FOUR GROUPS: COOL SEASON GRASSES; WARM SEASON GRASSES; MEMBERS OF THE DAISY FAMILY; AND MEMBERS OF THE PEA FAMILY.

WATCHING THE GRASS GROW

When you think of grass, the first thing that comes to mind is a lawn. But most lawn grasses are quite different from those that blanket the tallgrass prairie. Lawn grasses never grow very tall nor very tough. And as long as they are cut and watered, they stay green. Prairie grasses, however, grow for a certain amount of time and then send up their flower stalks. After the seeds form, the aboveground parts of the plants dry out. Some grasses are annuals and die after producing seeds. But the most common tallgrass species are perennials. The tops of these grasses die back in the fall. Their roots and buds, however, remain alive and grow again in the spring. A perennial grass plant can live ten to twenty years.

When a grass seed sprouts, it sends a tiny root down into the ground and a small green shoot upward toward the sun. As the shoot produces leaves that gather the sun's energy and the root collects water and minerals, the plant grows. The stem grows taller, putting out leaf blades along its length.

As they grow, some grasses send out stems that grow along the surface, called stolons. Stolons send down rootlets from their growing tips.

Underground stems called rhizomes also grow from the parent plant. Rhizomes have swollen joints along their length. Rootlets and new stems grow from the rhizome's joints and tip. Over time, the new roots and stems form a dense mat of grass called sod.

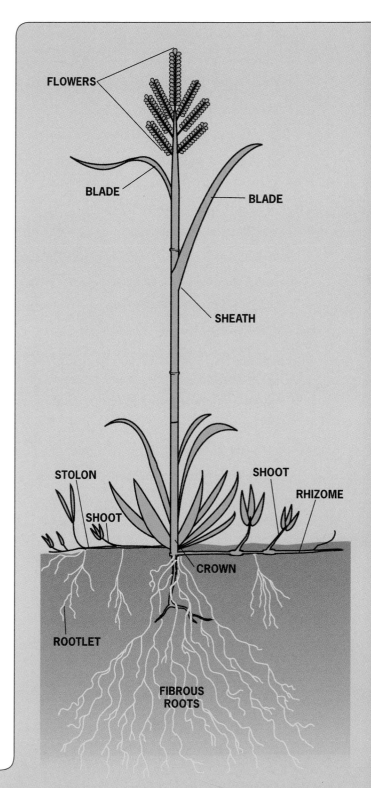

PRIMARY PRODUCERS: BIG FOUR GRASSES

About 150 different grass species live in the tallgrass prairie, but 4 species of grasses dominate all the others. All 4 can also be found growing in other places, but the tallgrass prairie is where they grow most abundantly.

Big bluestem (*Andropogon gerardii*) is the tallest. Where there's plenty of rainfall, big bluestem can form a thick, almost uniform blanket across large stretches of prairie. While it is most common on the prairie, this grass grows all the way from Maine to Florida. It extends to the west as far as Arizona and eastern Montana.

Despite its name, big bluestem shows many colors besides a bluish green. Depending on the season, it can be lead gray, tan, bronze, and even dark red. It normally grows 6 to 8 feet (about 2 meters) tall. But when the soil is moist and rich, its flower stalks can reach up to 12 feet (3.7 meters) in height. Some people call big bluestem turkey foot because the three branches of its seed head look like a turkey's foot. Where the soil is moist, big bluestem acts like a sod grass, sending out rhizomes that sprout new roots and leaves. But under drier conditions, it grows in bunchgrass clumps. The crowded stems help conserve moisture.

Little bluestem (*Andropogon scoparius*) is only little compared to its cousin, for it can reach 5 feet (nearly 2 meters) tall. It is more adaptable than big bluestem and can be found in all types of prairies. Little bluestem also grows in drier areas than its big cousin does. California, Nevada, Oregon, and Washington are the only western states where little bluestem doesn't grow.

Little bluestem usually grows in bunches. The shoots at the bottom of the plant are bluish, and the folded leaf blades are yellowish. In the fall, its golden tint colors huge patches of the prairie.

Indian grass (*Sorghastrum nutans*) makes beautiful, shiny, golden brown plumes atop tall stems. Under favorable conditions, it can grow as tall as big bluestem. Its leaves point upward at a 45-degree angle from the stem. Indian grass can adapt to different amounts of moisture and can be found in all parts of the prairie. Its range is much bigger than that of big bluestem, too. It grows southeast from the tallgrass prairie into Florida; north into Manitoba, Canada; and westward into Texas and Wyoming. Indian grass is especially hardy and can survive drought and extremes of temperature.

Switchgrass (*Panicum virgatum*) has curly leaves that grow in bunches. Tiny clusters of small hairs grow where the leaf blade attaches to the stem. Its delicate branched seed heads nod gracefully in the wind, and its yellow clumps survive through the winter. Switchgrass has the largest range of the big four grasses and lives throughout the United States except in the Pacific Coast states.

If you have ever dug up a crabgrass plant, you've seen how one grass plant can use these tough stems to multiply very quickly into a dense sod.

Some kinds of grasses, called bunchgrasses, make shoots called tillers right from the crown of the mother plant instead of sending out stolons or rhizomes. Bunchgrasses form tight clumps. They tend to grow where it is too dry for sod-forming grasses to grow.

A key to the success of grasses is the way they grow. Trees and most other plants, such as roses and other familiar garden flowers, have their growing tips at the ends of the branches and their buds at the bases of the leaves. The youngest cells are at the tips of the shoots. When a grazing animal feeds on them, the growing tips are eaten. If a young tree seedling is nipped off by a grazing animal, it dies because it has lost the part that can grow. Grasses, however, evolved to cope with grazers. Their growing tips are protected because they are at the base of the plant's stem. The oldest part of a grass leaf is at the tip. When the leaves are eaten, the growing part at the base of the stem is not disturbed. It can send up new leafy growth quickly. In addition, the young shoots are protected by being wrapped up inside the hollow older shoots.

Prairies are very productive ecosystems. With no trees to shade them, the thin blades of grass capture the sun's energy very efficiently. In the middle of the summer, 1 acre (0.4 hectares) of prairie can have up to 10 acres (4 hectares) of leaf surface area exposed to the light. All of those leaves soak up energy and lock it up in carbohydrates that can be used by both the plants and by the animals that eat the plants.

GRASSES THAT GROW IN CLUMPS ARE CALLED BUNCHGRASSES.

FORBS OF THE PRAIRIE

So many members of the daisy family live on the prairie that the daisy family is considered a characteristic of the tallgrass. Each blossom of a daisy family flower is actually a collection of many small flowers. The flowers around the outside of the blossom have long petals on one side. These are the petals you notice that form a circle around the center of the blossom. The other petals are small. The tiny flowers on the inside of the blossom have only very small petals that you don't usually notice.

The purple coneflower races with the cool season grasses, sending up its flower stalks to bloom above the tops of the growing grass. Purple coneflowers, which can be nearly 4 feet (over 1 meter) tall, bloom from late spring into midsummer. Unlike most flowers in the daisy family, the coneflower's center is cone shaped instead of flat.

Several kinds of sunflowers, which are in the daisy family, grow among the tallgrass. Wild sunflowers have bright yellow petals, but their centers can be yellow, brown, or purplish. Sunflowers bloom in late summer. If you look closely

PURPLE CONEFLOWERS BLOOM ABOVE THE PRAIRIE GRASSES.

GIANT SUNFLOWERS (*HELIANTHUS GIGANTEUS*)

at a sunflower blossom, you can easily see the many tiny flowers that make up the center. Sunflowers grow well on the prairie because they send up a shoot that can grow as fast as the grass and not be overshadowed by it. Sunflower seeds are important food for many kinds of birds.

Many kinds of legumes are found in the tallgrass, including larkspur and wild lupine. At least three species of clover are common here, too. The leadplant is a large, shrublike legume that lives in the uplands of the tallgrass. It can tolerate dry soil because its roots can plunge 4 feet (over 1 meter) into the ground. The leadplant has small grayish leaves and long spikes of small blue flowers.

FLOWERS ON THE PRAIRIE

When a grass plant is fully grown, it sends up a flower stalk. The flowers of grasses are not big and colorful. Unlike most flowering plants, grasses don't depend on bees or butterflies to pollinate their flowers. Instead, grasses are pollinated by the wind. Each bunch of flowers produces abundant pollen. If you look at a head of grass flowers when the pollen is ripe, you can see little yellow bits hanging from the flowers. The yellow color comes from the pollen.

Wind carries the pollen to the flowers of other grass plants. There, the pollen sticks to the female parts of the flower and pollinates it. The seeds grow, and the plant dries out. Some grass seeds simply fall to the ground to sprout, but others attach themselves to the fur of passing animals to be deposited far from the parent plant.

Many prairie forbs produce beautiful wildflowers. They depend on insects to act as pollinators, carrying pollen from one

SPIDERWORT (TRADESCANTIA) IS A LOVELY PRAIRIE WILDFLOWER.

flower to another. Their bright colors help attract the insects, which feed on pollen or sweet nectar from the flowers.

You can often tell by the shape or color of the flowers which insects are the usual pollinators. The bright orange clusters of butterfly weed provide a place for butterflies to land while they sip nectar from the flowers. Other flowers butterflies love also grow in clumps that provide landing platforms. Many flowers pollinated by bees look white to us. But bees can see ultraviolet light, which people can't, and the white flowers often have bright ultraviolet colors. Some clovers are pollinated by bumblebees. The nectar of these flowers is deep inside, where some kinds of bees can't reach it but bumblebees can.

Other animals find ways to use flowers to get food, too. Crab spiders hide on prairie flowers and nab insects that visit to collect pollen and nectar. The front legs of these spiders curve forward so they can quickly grab their prey. Their color varies, depending on the color of the flower they live on, which makes it easy for them to hide from their prey.

LIFE AMONG THE GRASSES

Primary consumers of the tallgrass include a great variety of animals, from insects to bison, that gain nourishment from the prairie grasses and forbs. On the Osage Prairie in northeastern Oklahoma, 65 percent of all the invertebrate animals—those without a backbone—feed on plants. Even though countless millions of leaf eaters, such as grasshoppers, and plant-juice feeders, such as aphids, may live on a prairie, the plants grow so well under the hot sun that the consumers normally have little impact.

The environment varies enormously at different heights above the ground. At ground level, it's cool and dark, and the air is still. No more than 3 percent of the sunlight reaches this shadowy region of the tallgrass. If an ant were climbing a grass stem from the ground up on a sunny summer day, the amount of moisture would lessen as the amount of light increased. Soon, the ant would be swaying back and forth with the stem it was climbing, blown by the prairie wind. As the ant neared the top of the stem, it would emerge into the bright light and intense heat of summer.

PRIMARY CONSUMER: GRASSHOPPER

Grasshoppers are well named, for grasslands everywhere are their true home. These primary consumers are well adapted for life among the grasses, and hundreds of species live on American prairies.

Grasshoppers are built for jumping. A grasshopper's third pair of legs are very long and are bent in the middle. By pushing off powerfully with these hind legs, a grasshopper can jump twenty to thirty times its own length.

Many familiar insects, such as butterflies and beetles, go through what is called complete metamorphosis. Their eggs hatch into larvae, worm-shaped creatures that look nothing like the adults. Insects have a hard outer shell called an exoskeleton. As they grow, they shed the old exoskeleton and a new, larger one then hardens. A butterfly larva, or caterpillar, sheds its skin and grows, finally developing into a chrysalis, a nonmoving stage that is attached to vegetation. Inside the chrysalis, the adult butterfly develops. When it is ready, it breaks through the chrysalis wall and emerges as a butterfly.

Grasshoppers and some other insects have incomplete metamorphosis. Grasshoppers lay their eggs in moist soil. Each egg hatches into a nymph, which looks similar to the adult but has no wings. The nymph grows and sheds its skin several times, looking more and more like the adult. After the last molt, the grasshopper has fully grown wings and can fly. Some grasshoppers have bright red or yellow wings, but others have plain green or brown ones.

Some kinds of grasshoppers can undergo a strange change when they are crowded. When young grasshoppers are exposed to large populations of their own kind, they develop longer wings, especially efficient muscles, and different colors. They change from stay-at-home loners into swarming, long distance travelers called locusts. Locusts are active and restless, taking to the wind in huge swarms.

In the past, grasshoppers that lived far from the tallgrass, in the dry, short grasses at the foot of the Rocky Mountains, sometimes changed into ravaging locusts when a series of years with favorable weather caused a population explosion. They rode the wind across the plains and attacked the tallgrass in countless numbers. These huge swarms of millions of locusts could completely consume large areas of the prairie.

Animals like voles and snakes live at or close to the surface of the ground. Small mammals, such as mice and voles, are common on the prairie. The meadow vole is found in all sorts of Midwestern and northern grasslands. These creatures make long tunnels through the grass at the surface. Even where the prairie is dense, voles can scurry through their tunnels quickly. Voles eat grass, roots, and seeds. Where trees grow, voles eat bark.

Slithering through the grass is easy for snakes, which have no legs to get in the way as they move between stems and stalks. Corn snakes, western ribbon snakes, prairie king snakes, and several kinds of garter snakes hunt voles and other rodents, as well as frogs, amidst the tallgrass. They also hunt on other kinds of grasslands.

The stems and leaves of prairie plants are home to many kinds of insects and spiders. Spiders are secondary consumers that feed on the insects that become trapped in their webs. Most prairie insects are primary consumers, feeding on different parts of prairie plants. Aphids and spittlebugs have special mouthparts that penetrate the stems of plants. They feed on plant juices. If you've ever noticed white clusters of bubbles that look like spit on plants, chances are you've seen the protective foam made by the spittlebug larva that protects it from predators and from dryness.

Many kinds of beetles live on the prairie. The potato beetle feeds on leaves of members of the potato family. The june beetle devours pollen and ripening fruit as well as leaves. Other beetles cluster on flowers and feed on the pollen.

Grasshoppers are the most common invertebrates on the prairie. They eat only about 20 percent of the grass they cut. The rest becomes part of the ground litter that is decomposed by other living things. But even in a dry year, the number of grasshoppers isn't great enough to cause real damage to the wild prairie.

(ABOVE) **THE TALLGRASS PRAIRIE PROVIDES PLENTY OF INSECT PREY FOR SPIDERS LIKE THIS ARGIOPE.**

(NEAR RIGHT) **SOME GRASSLAND BEETLES FEED ON POLLEN.**

PRAIRIE BIRDS

Most of the birds you might see on the tallgrass prairie, such as eastern meadowlarks and bobwhite quail, also live in other ecosystems. Most forest birds build their nests in trees, a convenient place that helps protect the chicks from many predators. Prairie birds, on the other hand, nest mostly on the ground or among the grasses. Some nest in shrubs or dense plants.

Grassland birds are often highly social and live in large flocks for much of the year. They have no branches to perch on, so they sing their lovely songs on the wing or while perched on the waving stalks of grasses or forbs.

One bird that needs undisturbed tallgrass or mixed grass prairie to survive is the greater prairie chicken. The males perform a complex courtship display to attract the females. Shortly before dawn, the male prairie chickens gather in areas where the grass is low. The males dance wildly about with their heads low and wings spread out. The bright orange air sacs in their necks help make loud, booming sounds to impress the females. The still dawn air carries their calls far without interference from the sound of the wind rustling the grass. Male prairie chickens have used the same areas over and over again for their "booming grounds," perhaps for hundreds of years.

YELLOW-HEADED BLACKBIRDS (*XANTHOCEPHALUS XANTHOCEPHALUS*) LIVE ON PRAIRIE MARSHES.

CHAPTER 3

LIFE UNDERGROUND

Deep roots are a major reason for the success of the tallgrass prairie. The tallgrass prairie is like the rain forest turned upside down. In the rain forest, almost all the life is above the ground. The trees and other plants have shallow roots, and the soil is not very fertile. The opposite is true of the prairie, which has far more of its living plant material below the ground than any kind of forest.

The amount of living material in an ecosystem is called its biomass. During a growing season, ecologists compared the aboveground and underground growth of plants in the Minnesota tallgrass prairie and an oak forest. The underground biomass of the oak forest was less than 10 percent of the total biomass. In the prairie, however, about 50 percent of the plants' biomass was underground. During the winter, almost all the tallgrass biomass remains below the surface.

NEAR THE SOIL'S SURFACE, 5 SQUARE FEET (0.5 SQUARE METERS) OF BIG BLUESTEM SOD CAN BE DENSELY PACKED WITH ALMOST 13 MILES (21 KILOMETERS) OF ROOTLETS AND ROOT HAIRS.

THE IMPORTANCE OF ROOTS

Grass roots can penetrate very deeply into the soil. Switchgrass roots can reach 11 feet (3.4 meters) into the ground. And although the stems and leaves of grasses are straight and unbranched, the roots have many tiny rootlets that branch off from the main roots. Millions to billions of tiny root hairs grow on the roots of each plant. The root hairs are microscopic. Their thin walls absorb water and minerals from the soil. Near the soil's surface, 5 square feet (0.5 square meters) of big bluestem sod can be densely packed with almost 13 miles (21 kilometers) of rootlets and root hairs.

Deep, dense roots are critical to survival in what is often a dry environment. In the tallgrass, most of the rain falls during the growing season, early summer to midsummer. By late summer, the rainfall is so slight that even when rain falls on the leaves and stems of the grass, little water reaches the ground. In a light shower, 97 percent of the water falling on a patch of big bluestem stays on the grass. Even in a heavy rain, only one third of the water gets to the soil. To survive, prairie grasses need lots of roots, and they must develop them while

they are very young. When a plant of big bluestem is seventy days old, the leaves reach up only about 8 inches (20 centimeters), but its branched root system already reaches 2 feet (0.6 meters) underground. At that time, the aboveground part of the plant can barely be seen.

These deep roots also store energy that helps the plants grow again in the spring or after being grazed, burned, or cut. The roots get help from a surprising source in their quest for minerals. Underground fungi form dense mats of extremely fine filaments that provide lots of surface area for absorbing minerals from the soil. The plant roots absorb the minerals from the fungi, and the fungi absorb sugars and other chemicals from the roots. This combination of plant roots and fungal strands is called a mycorrhiza.

(LEFT) **PRAIRIE GRASSES GROW MANY ROOTS.**

(ABOVE) **MYCORRHIZAE PROVIDE MINERALS TO PLANT ROOTS.**

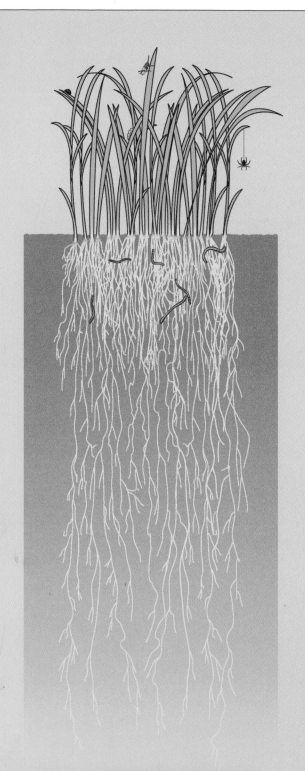

A grass plant's roots are also important storage organs for the carbohydrates the plant will need to fuel its growth in the spring. As the aboveground parts of prairie plants die in late summer and fall, carbohydrates are transferred from the leaves and stems into the roots for the winter. That way, when spring sunshine warms the ground, the plants have the energy to grow quickly.

Dead grass takes two to three years to decompose and become part of the soil. But the tallgrass prairie has been around for thousands of years. In some tallgrass areas, the topsoil is 20 feet (6 meters) deep, making it perhaps the most fertile soil in the world.

DECOMPOSING THE GRASS

The soil in the tallgrass prairie teems with life. In the top layer of soil, dead plants are constantly being broken down into simpler chemicals. The result is a dark, fluffy mixture called humus. A variety of living things, including nematode worms, fungi, and bacteria, carry out the work of decomposing plant material. A tiny pinch

GRASS ROOTS REACH DEEP INTO THE EARTH, GIVING THE TALLGRASS PRAIRIE AS MUCH BIOMASS UNDERGROUND AS ABOVE GROUND.

DECOMPOSER: EARTHWORM

The earthworm is the unsung hero of grasslands. Earthworms feed on bits of dead matter and turn them into material that can be used by plants. Scientists use the term *detritivore* to describe this mode of feeding.

Almost five million earthworms tunnel and feed under just 1 acre (0.4 hectares) of tallgrass at Konza Prairie Research Natural Area. Such large numbers of animals have important effects on the soil. Earthworms do a great deal to mix it up. They pull leaves from the surface down into their burrows. They move deeper soil to the top when they deposit their digestive waste, called castings, on the surface. Earthworms bring from 2 to 100 tons (2 to 90 metric tons) of material to the surface of 1 acre (0.4 hectares) of land in a year, depending on the soil and climate.

Because of this activity, stones and other objects lying on the ground are gradually buried as earthworms pull soil out from underneath and deposit it on top. Over a few years, several inches of soil may be deposited on top of things that used to be lying on the surface. Earthworms are a major cause of the burying of ancient cities and monuments.

Earthworms' activities help improve the soil. When earthworms pull leaves into their burrows, shred them, digest them, and deposit the remains, they are making valuable nutrients available to plants. Their tunnels allow air and water to penetrate soil more easily and provide easy channels for root growth. The castings and the decaying leaves lining the burrows also nourish the roots.

of humus can be home to fifty-eight million tiny bacteria.

Breaking down organic matter isn't the only service the bacteria perform. They help make the element nitrogen available for other living things. In addition to carbon dioxide, water, and other simple inorganic chemicals, life requires nitrogen. All proteins contain nitrogen, and proteins are vital to the survival of all living things. Enzymes—molecules that help bring about the chemical reactions of life—are proteins, as is the hemoglobin that carries oxygen in the blood. Proteins help make up the walls and vital membranes of cells, and the muscles of animals are made largely of protein.

Certain bacteria in the soil are able to take nitrogen gas from the air and incorporate it into their cells, making it available to other living things. This process is called nitrogen fixation. The most efficient of these bacteria live in the roots of legumes, which have small swellings, called nodules, on their roots where the bacteria live. The nitrogen-fixing bacteria that live in the nodules make much more nitrogen available to plants than do free-living bacteria. Only 7 to 13 percent of

CLOVER IS A LEGUME WITH ROOT NODULES THAT FIX NITROGEN.

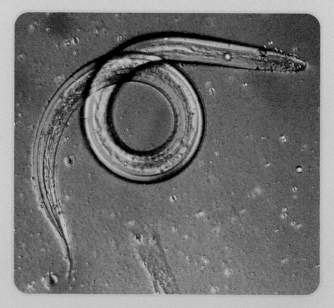

NEMATODE WORMS (CAENORHABDITIS ELEGANS, SHOWN HERE) ARE VERY COMMON IN PRAIRIE SOILS.

nitrogen fixed by free-living bacteria is released into the soil, while more than 90 percent of the nitrogen fixed within root nodules can be used by the plant.

Nitrogen-fixing bacteria take nitrogen from the air pockets in the soil and combine it with hydrogen to make ammonia. The bacteria use some of the ammonia for their own growth and metabolism, but most of the ammonia goes to the legume. Then, when animals eat the legumes, they use that same nitrogen for their own growth. In return for nitrogen it can use, the legume provides the bacteria with a place to live. The nodules also protect the bacteria from too much oxygen, which can break down their nitrogen-fixing enzyme. A special chemical in the nodule that is similar to the hemoglobin in our blood holds onto the oxygen, giving it up to the bacteria in small quantities only when needed.

ANIMALS UNDERGROUND

The ground underneath the tallgrass makes an excellent home for some interesting forms of life besides the countless microscopic creatures. The most common animals in the prairie soil are roundworms, or nematodes. Most soil nematodes are so tiny you wouldn't notice them in a pinch of soil. You'd need a hand lens to see them clearly. Many kinds of nematodes live in the thin film of water surrounding soil particles. They feed on bacteria. Others suck plant juices or feed on the roots. Nematodes may consume more biomass below the ground than grazers do above the ground.

Some bigger animals also live underground in tallgrass prairies. Franklin's ground squirrel is one of the few mammals that spends most of its life in underground tunnels. It does come to the surface to feed on grasshoppers and shrews. This grayish animal lives only in tallgrass and mixed prairies, where the tall, dense grass hides the entrance to its burrow. It looks similar to a gray tree squirrel, but has a shorter tail and smaller ears.

The plains pocket gopher spends even less time above ground than Franklin's ground squirrel, only emerging from its burrow when it is young and during the mating season. Otherwise, it is found underground, living in a maze of branching tunnels that can be almost 100 feet (30 meters) long, with side chambers for storing food, defecating, and raising young. This secretive animal has an abundant food source—the roots of plants, mostly grass. It has big, sharp front teeth that close in front of its lips, keeping dirt from getting into its mouth. The long, sharp claws on its front feet are efficient for digging, aided if necessary by the front teeth.

Living underground doesn't hide the plains pocket gopher completely from predators, however. The badger is a powerful digging hunter that lives in the prairie and preys on pocket gophers. The badger uses the long, curved, sharp claws on its front feet for digging and its shovel-shaped hind feet for pushing out the dirt it excavates.

To hunt pocket gophers, a badger finds a burrow, then digs a series of holes along the burrow's length. Using its sense of smell to try to locate the gopher, the badger enters one of its vertical tunnels, then explores along the gopher's burrow looking for its prey. If it fails to find the pocket gopher, the badger comes back to the surface, chooses another one of the holes it has dug, and descends again.

LIFE ABOUNDS ALONG THE PRAIRIE EDGES.

CHAPTER 4
LIVING ON THE EDGE

The tallgrass meets up with a number of different habitats. Most tallgrass plants and animals also live in the mixed grass prairie to the west. The tallgrass also borders on areas with trees and with waterways such as ponds, lakes, marshes, streams, and rivers.

The "edge effect" refers to the special abundance of different life-forms in the areas where two ecosystems meet. Plants and animals from both ecosystems are present. In addition, some other plants and animals are specially adapted to living along such boundary lines. The edge effect is especially strong in the tallgrass prairie, making it an ecosystem of abundant biodiversity. It has a great variety of different species of living things.

FROM FOREST TO FIELD

Climatic conditions in southern Michigan and Wisconsin favor the growth of bur oaks scattered through the prairie bordering the eastern forest. A grassland with scattered trees is called a savanna. The trees in such a savanna are quite evenly spaced, like trees in an orchard, far enough apart that their branches usually don't touch, even when full grown.

Trees and prairies can form other combinations, too. In some places, prairie grasses surround a stand of trees. In others,

the opposite is true—the grassland is surrounded by forest. In many areas, the forest gradually thins, with oaks, hickories, or maples gradually petering out until there is only prairie. Trees also grow along the borders of the waterways of the prairie.

Along the edges of the forest, shrubs and small trees that need both light and shade, such as sumac and chokecherries, can form a transition between the trees and grasses. Forbs that cannot survive in the heavy shade of the forest or the bright, unrelenting sun of the prairie also thrive along the borderline between forest and prairie.

In some places, the forest ends quite abruptly in a zone of shrubby growth, such as wild plums and crabapples, then dogwood and hazel draped by wild grapevines. A narrow band of sunflowers edges the shrubs,

then the tallgrass spreads out for miles and miles to the west.

ANIMALS ALONG THE EDGES OF THE FOREST

White-tailed deer favor open forests that border grasslands, including the tallgrass prairie. Whitetails are cautious creatures that prefer the cover of the forest. But much of their food—especially in the springtime when they feed on the tender new growth of forbs—is in the grassland. White-tailed deer tend to spend the daylight hours hidden in the forest, leaving its protection at dusk to feed in the open.

Whitetail fawns are born in late spring, and the mothers often leave the fawns bedded down among the grasses while they go off to feed. The spotted fawns are well camouflaged in the deep

MANY BIRDS FEED ON THE PRAIRIE BUT NEED TREES TO NEST. LIKE THE WHITE-TAILED DEER, THEY ARE FOUND MOST COMMONLY ALONG THE EDGES OF THE FORESTS AND WATERWAYS.

grass. They can lie completely still, curled up and hidden in the grass, for hours at a time.

Many birds feed in the prairie but need trees to nest. Like the white-tailed deer, they are found most commonly along the edges of the forests and waterways. The bright yellow American goldfinch is a typical bird of the forest edge. It builds its nest in trees or tall shrubs. This beautiful bird is found along the edges of the tallgrass prairie from north to south. It flits between forest and grassland, nesting in trees but feeding in the open on seeds of grassland plants. The lovely eastern bluebird feeds on insects and fruit rather than seeds, but it requires a tree hole for nesting.

Cliff and barn swallows live along the edges of all sorts of American grasslands. They need cliffs and rocky ledges along streams and rivers to build their nests, but the prairie provides an abundance of the flying insects that are the swallows' food.

The fox squirrel would rather live where the prairie meets the forest than in the deep woods. It feeds more on the ground than its cousin, the gray squirrel. The ribbons of riverbank forests that wind through the prairie are a favorite habitat of the fox squirrel. This largest tree squirrel makes a large nest of leaves in a tree during the summer and lives in a tree hole in winter. It remains active during the winter, eating nuts it had buried earlier.

LIVING BY THE WATER

A great variety of life makes its home around the edges of prairie ponds, marshes, and lakes. Where the prairie is

WHITE-TAILED DEER *(ODOCOILEUS VIRGINIANUS)* PREFER TO LIVE IN WOODS AND THICKETS ON THE EDGES OF GRASSLANDS.

relatively flat, the border of a pond can offer several different habitats for plants, depending on the distance from the shore. The closer to the pond, the wetter the habitat. Some grasses, such as prairie cordgrass, do best in very damp soil. And right at the edge of a pond or marsh, water-loving plants like cattails live.

Parts of the northern tallgrass are dotted by shallow ponds called prairie potholes, which provide homes for many different living things. Waterfowl, such as canvasback ducks and blue-winged teal, feed on aquatic plants and breed in prairie potholes. Ducks and geese nest in the grass around the pothole. The mottled brown feathers of a mother duck disguise her well. When the ducklings hatch, she leads them to the water, where they spend most of their lives.

Birds that feed on insects and other invertebrates make their homes among the cattails and along the shore. These include red-winged blackbirds, marsh wrens, and sora rails.

Several species of frogs, toads, and salamanders depend on ponds for breeding. Many insects, such as dragonflies and mosquitoes, also breed in prairie potholes.

PONDS PROVIDE HOMES FOR MANY PLANTS AND ANIMALS.

SECONDARY CONSUMER: BULL SNAKE

Like most of the living things in the tallgrass prairie, the secondary consumers are not limited to this ecosystem. A number of snakes venture into the grasses in search of prey, especially the bull snake *(Pituopis melanoleucus)*.

Most snakes are silent, but the bull snake gives a loud warning hiss when disturbed that can be heard from 50 feet (15 meters) away. The sound is impressive—it sounds like the bellow of a bull. The bull snake also vibrates its tail when alarmed, striking it against dry leaves to make a sound similar to a rattlesnake's rattle.

This powerful creature is one of North America's largest snakes and can reach 8 feet or more (nearly 3 meters) in length. Its body ranges in color from straw brown to an orange yellow. Rows of square reddish brown or black blotches mark its back and sides. It lives in the western part of the tallgrass and westward through mixed and short-grass prairie to the Rocky Mountains. It eats mostly rodents, especially ground squirrels, pursuing them in their underground burrows. Bull snakes may also feed on birds and their eggs. The bull snake is not poisonous—it is a constrictor, killing its prey by squeezing it or pressing it against a solid object, such as the walls of a burrow.

MIGRATING THROUGH THE TALLGRASS

In spring and fall, the tallgrass and its waterways provide vital stopping places for migrating birds. Many kinds of birds breed in the north and then fly south to spend the winter in milder climates. Along the way, they stop to feed and rest in the prairie and along the rivers that pass through it.

At least 40 percent of North American shorebirds and waterfowl migrate along the Mississippi Flyway between their breeding grounds in the north and their winter homes in Central and South America. The flyway follows the Mississippi River and therefore runs right through the tallgrass prairie. Birds that breed as far north as the arctic coast of Alaska and those that winter as far south as Patagonia, at the southern tip of South America, pass along the Mississippi Flyway. Ducks, geese, shorebirds, blackbirds, sparrows, warblers, and thrushes all use it. As they travel, the tallgrass prairie provides them with the nourishment they need for their long journey.

MIGRATORY BIRDS LIKE SNOW GEESE (CHEN CAERULESCENS)
PASS THROUGH THE PRAIRIE EVERY SPRING AND FALL.

CHAPTER 5
BIODIVERSITY

The American tallgrass prairie is home to many different species of living things, and thus is a center of great biodiversity because it includes so many habitats. Areas like the prairie potholes, which provide different kinds of habitats right near each other, are "patchy"—they are made up of patches of different kinds of plants. The different kinds of plants encourage more animal species, too, so a patchy habitat usually contains more biodiversity than a uniform one.

The tallgrass is patchy in many different ways. The dips between prairie hills and knolls provide deep, thick areas of very tall grasses, while the tops of the hills have shorter, less dense stands of grass. Trees growing along the edges of the prairie provide cover, food, and nesting sites for many kinds of birds and

THE MANY HABITATS OF THE KANSAS TALLGRASS ARE HOME TO DIVERSE COMMUNITIES OF PLANTS AND ANIMALS.

mammals that otherwise wouldn't be able to inhabit the prairie.

The wetlands of the prairie provide the greatest boost to its biodiversity. Not only do trees grow along waterways, an abundance of every kind of life from bacteria to mammals inhabits prairie ponds, lakes, marshes, streams, and rivers.

THE VITAL BISON

One animal more than any other plays a vital role in maintaining biodiversity in the tallgrass prairie. Bison are natives of all three kinds of prairie ecosystems—tallgrass, mixed, and short-grass. Traveling through the dense tallgrass is no problem for these massive creatures.

Bison influence all aspects of prairie ecology through their activities. By grazing, bison help maintain plant diversity. These large grazers prefer grass to forbs. Grass makes up about 90 percent of their diet. In areas where grass grows thickly, bison keep the grass relatively short. When the grass has been eaten, it must put its energy into growing back rather than to spreading. Bison grazing thus helps keep the grasses in check, so they don't overwhelm the forbs. Without bison, grass can take over, producing a prairie with few forbs.

Where bison graze, forbs are able to grow vigorously, with less competition from the grass. When the forbs die back in the fall, they leave behind more dead plant material than the grazed grasses do. So when the prairie burns, it burns unevenly. The fire blackens the areas where the forbs grew but may skip the places where bison consumed the grass. The burned, dead leaves and

> NOT ONLY DO TREES GROW ALONG WATERWAYS, AN ABUNDANCE OF EVERY KIND OF LIFE FROM BACTERIA TO MAMMALS INHABITS PRAIRIE PONDS, LAKES, MARSHES, STREAMS, AND RIVERS.

(ABOVE) **A LONE BULL BISON**
(BISON BISON)

(LEFT) **BISON HAVE THICK, DARK FUR ON THEIR HEADS.**

stems of the forbs provide fertilizer for new growth, helping keep the forbs strong and healthy.

A variety of species of grasses and forbs encourages a similar variety of animals that have different requirements for food and habitat. While bison prefer to eat grass, some other animals, such as white-tailed deer, eat mostly forbs. Some insects specialize in eating grass, while others feast on forbs.

Bison increase prairie biodiversity in other ways. They have a habit of wallowing in mud and rolling in dust to keep insects from biting them. The animals paw at the ground as they roll, exposing the soil and killing the plants. Over time, these "buffalo wallows" become areas with no plants, up to 20 feet (5 meters) in diameter and 10 inches (30 centimeters) deep. When it's rainy, the wallows fill with water, allowing short-lived aquatic organisms, such as algae and mosquito larvae, to grow. In summer the wallows become very dry. When the bison abandon a wallow, only plants that tolerate drought well can grow there. Annual grasses and forbs that have a

WHEN BISON TAKE DUST BATHS, THEY KILL PERENNIAL PLANTS,
LEAVING A PLACE FOR ANNUAL PLANTS TO GROW.

difficult time competing with perennials can sprout and grow on the bare ground of the wallows.

PRODUCTIVITY AND DIVERSITY

Bison grazing increases the productivity of the prairie. When the tall grasses are eaten, more light can reach all the plants, providing them with more energy to grow. The growing grass is also more nutritious because nitrogen stored in the roots moves into the leaves when they are actively growing, instead of being locked away in roots below the ground. In this way, the nutrients become available to grazing animals from grasshoppers to bison.

Many prairie animals don't need to drink water. They are able to use the water their bodies can capture from their food to meet their needs. But bison have to drink water to survive. They travel to rivers, lakes, and ponds to drink. Then they come back into the grasslands, bringing that water with them and contributing it to the prairie through their urine. The urine of bison and other animals also adds nitrogen to the soil. When a bison defecates, it adds still more organic matter to the ground, which acts to fertilize the plants. Dung beetles and other insects feed on the bison feces, bolstering the biodiversity of the prairie and breaking down the feces further, making them more usable for prairie plants.

A bison bull can weigh nearly 2,000 pounds (800 kilograms). When it dies, its body is a source of food for many organisms. Bison hide is tough, so the first scavengers on the scene are birds like bald eagles and vultures that have strong beaks to penetrate the bison skin. Then coyotes and magpies, ravens, and other birds can join in. Meanwhile, flies lay their eggs on the carcass, and worms, bacteria, and fungi feed. The high nitrogen content of the fluids released as the carcass decomposes kills plants at first. But in a few years, the nitrogen content is just right for fertilizing plants. Then the aboveground primary production where bison carcasses are decomposing reaches two or three times that of undisturbed prairie.

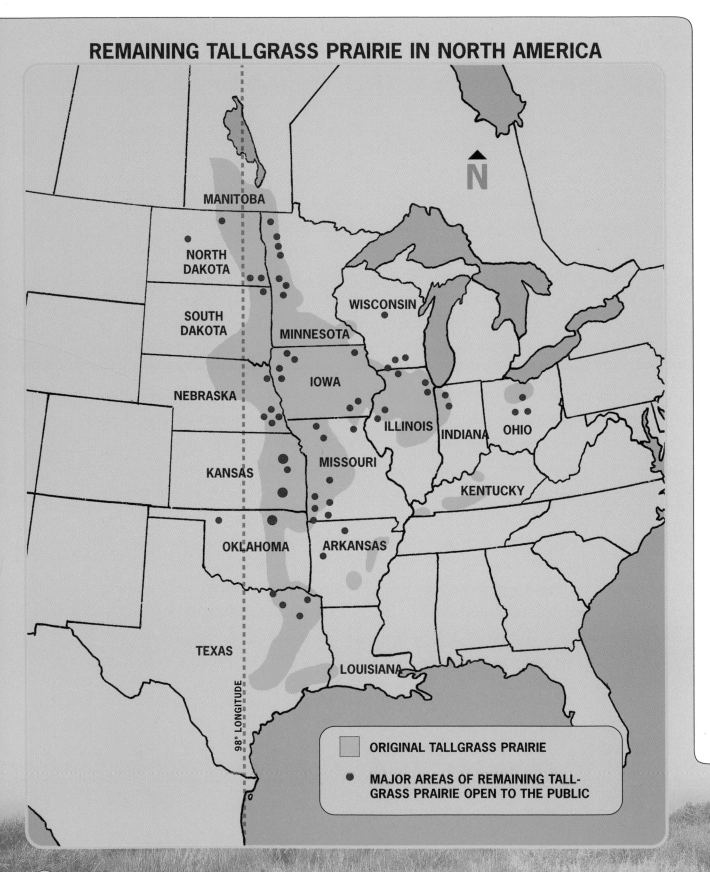

REMAINING TALLGRASS PRAIRIE IN NORTH AMERICA

MANITOBA

NORTH DAKOTA

SOUTH DAKOTA

MINNESOTA

WISCONSIN

NEBRASKA

IOWA

ILLINOIS

INDIANA

OHIO

KANSAS

MISSOURI

KENTUCKY

OKLAHOMA

ARKANSAS

TEXAS

LOUISIANA

98° LONGITUDE

N

ORIGINAL TALLGRASS PRAIRIE

MAJOR AREAS OF REMAINING TALL-GRASS PRAIRIE OPEN TO THE PUBLIC

CHAPTER 6
PEOPLE AND THE PRAIRIE

Long before Europeans came to North America, Native Americans lived and hunted on the prairie. Prairie tribes were generally nomads, moving from place to place to follow the herds of animals they depended on. Without Plains Indians, the tallgrass prairie probably would not have occupied as much territory. The prairie's abundance of bison, deer, and elk provided good hunting. To encourage the growth of tender grass to nourish these grazers, the Indians set fire to the prairie. The fires killed tree seedlings and maintained the prairie.

INDIANS AND BISON

The bison was the most important animal to the Plains Indians. Just about every part of the animal was used. The meat was lean and nutritious. Buffalo blood became pudding or soup. The tough hides made durable tepees and warm robes, clothing, and moccasins. Tendons were turned into tough thread and bowstrings. Bison wool was used to insulate moccasins and stuff dolls, and for weaving blankets. Arrow points, drinking cups, utensils, and many other items were made from buffalo horns. Hooves became spoons and glue, while bones were fashioned into different tools—war clubs, knife handles, arrowheads, and so forth. Bones even became runners for small sleds pulled by dogs. Bison teeth were valued as ornaments for clothing and jewelry. Bison stomachs were dried and used as canteens for water, as were the membranes surrounding the animal's heart and bladder. Nothing was wasted.

ARRIVAL OF EUROPEANS

Until 1803, the United States extended only as far as the Mississippi River. The only part of the prairie open to settlers was in Indiana and Illinois. But in 1803, President Thomas Jefferson acquired the entire midsection of the continent from France in the Louisiana Purchase, and a great change occurred. The prairie became part of the United States.

Europeans and their descendants who had lived in forested eastern North America were amazed by the tallgrass prairie. They had never seen anything like it. Europe and eastern North America had forests, rivers, and grassy hills. But here was grass, grass, grass, as far as they could see, with no relief from the blazing sun. Because the prairie lacked trees, early travelers and settlers thought the soil must be infertile. How wrong they were! But their assumptions weren't the only thing in the way of using the prairie for farmland. The dense, deep, tough mat of roots could barely be penetrated by the plows available in the early 1800s.

WHAT WAS ONCE TALLGRASS PRAIRIE BECAME ONE OF THE RICHEST AGRICULTURAL REGIONS ON THE EARTH.

Around 1820, however, grassland settlement began. The trickle of settlers that began in the 1820s grew to a torrent in the 1830s, after a new steel plow was developed that could cut through the dense tallgrass sod. By the 1840s, most of the grasslands of Indiana and Illinois had been plowed under. Within another thirty-five years, the majority of the tallgrass prairie had disappeared.

The earliest settlers were able to claim land on the edge of the woods or along streams. When all wooded tracts were gone, only grass was left. How could a home be built without wood? The ingenious settlers solved the problem by using the prairie itself to build their homes. Their rugged houses were made from slabs of the prairie sod and were called soddies. The slabs were cut about 4 inches

(10 centimeters) thick, 2.5 feet (76 centimeters) wide, and 3 to 4 feet (about 1 meter) long. Each slab weighed about 50 pounds (20 kilograms). The slabs were laid grass-side-down in layers to form walls. Holes were left for windows and doors. Mud filled any gaps between the slabs of sod.

A soddy had both disadvantages and advantages compared to a wooden house. Mice, snakes, and other animals sometimes tunneled in, and the uneven dirt floor was hard to keep clean. But the soddy was fireproof, an important trait on the fire-prone prairie. And the thick walls insulated the home well, holding in warmth in winter and coolness in summer.

Settlers on the tallgrass prairie found that it made fine farmland. Over the ages, the decomposing plants had created a thick, rich layer of soil perfect for growing corn and other crops. Once the grass and its roots had been conquered, the ground was easy to work, for rocks were few and far between. What was once tallgrass prairie became one of the richest agricultural regions on the earth.

As European settlement spread across

THE HOMES OF PRAIRIE SETTLERS WERE MADE OF PRAIRIE SOD AND WERE CALLED SODDIES.

the central plains of North America, crops to feed the growing population of people and domesticated animals replaced the wild grasses and other prairie plants. Corn, itself a grass that grows very tall, replaced tallgrass prairie.

Only about 2 percent of the original tallgrass prairie remains. Many of the animals typical of the prairie, such as the buffalo wolf, disappeared along with the plants. What was once the tallgrass prairie is now called the Corn Belt, the Midwest region where corn can be grown without irrigation.

DISAPPEARING PLANTS AND ANIMALS

Because few people recognized the beauty and importance of the tallgrass prairie and because its soil is perhaps the most fertile on earth, the tallgrass prairie has gone from being one of the most widespread American ecosystems to one of its rarest and most fragmented. It is the ecosystem most in danger of disappearing completely.

With their home plowed under, prairie plants and animals had no place to go. Farmland with crops and pastures covered

CORN HARVEST ON FORMER TALLGRASS PRAIRIE IN IOWA

what once had been tallgrass, and cities and towns dotted the landscape. Not only had people destroyed the prairie, they had interfered with the processes that could have helped any undeveloped grassland survive. No longer could fires sweep across miles and miles of grass, killing tree seedlings. The remaining bits of prairie weren't connected to one another, and people did what they could to stop any fires that started. Trees were able to root where they hadn't grown before, taking over much of the remaining grassland and replacing prairie with forest.

Fortunately, most species that thrive in the tallgrass prairie can also live in other habitats. White-tailed deer, for example, are just as comfortable in a woodland bordering a farmer's field as in the prairie. Some of the few plants and animals that can live only in the tallgrass and mixed prairie are now rare, and some are endangered. The greater prairie chicken, for example, once ranged through most of the tallgrass and parts of the mixed prairie. Now only scattered populations survive.

Several tallgrass flowers are endangered or threatened today. The

(NEAR LEFT) **MOST TALLGRASS PRAIRIE HAS BEEN TURNED INTO FARMS AND PASTURES.**

(ABOVE) **DAISY FLEABANE *(ERIGERON STRIGOSUS)* GROWS ALONG RAILROAD RIGHTS-OF-WAY.**

eastern and the western prairie fringed orchid, Mead's milkweed, prairie bush clover, and northern wild monkshood are threatened. Running buffalo clover is endangered.

Most tallgrass species that survived managed to do so by living along railroad rights-of-way. Along each side of railroad tracks runs a strip of uncultivated land, and wild plants can grow there undisturbed. The Flint Hills of Kansas also remain largely as tallgrass prairie, for they lie on a shallow layer of rocky soil and were never plowed. A few other patches of tallgrass also remain here and there.

FUTURE OF THE TALLGRASS

Until recently, people didn't value the prairie. When land was set aside for parks and preserves, it usually featured spectacular mountains or colorful rocky desert. Grasslands didn't seem like a place to inspire people. Many people still don't appreciate the prairie. Every year, more bits and pieces of it are destroyed to make way for homes, roads, and shopping malls.

Conservationists know that people need to learn about and preserve all kinds of ecosystems and the plants and animals that live in them in order to live on a healthy planet. It is difficult for scientists to study the true tallgrass prairie. The bits and pieces that are left are all small fragments of what was once an enormous region. An important principle of biology is that when an ecosystem is broken into small pieces, a great deal of its biodiversity disappears. This is certainly true of the tallgrass prairie.

THE KONZA PRAIRIE IS A PROTECTED AREA WHERE TALLGRASS
CAN THRIVE AND SCIENTISTS CAN STUDY PRAIRIE LIFE.

Scientists are able to study some aspects of the tallgrass prairie, however. The Nature Conservancy now owns and protects 8,000 acres (about 3,000 hectares) of the Flint Hills, called the Konza Prairie Research Natural Area. In 1987 thirty bison were reintroduced to the Konza Prairie, the largest area of unplowed tallgrass in the country that is used for research. The bison thrive in their native habitat. By 1992 about two hundred of them wandered over the gentle hills of the Konza Prairie. Since then, people at the Konza Prairie have kept the number of bison steady at around two hundred.

In 1989 the Nature Conservancy bought almost 30,000 acres (about 10,000 hectares) of ranchland near Pawhuska, Oklahoma, to add to 6,000 acres (about 2,000 hectares) that it already owned. This Tallgrass Prairie Preserve is the Nature Conservancy's largest project. Even though the land had never been plowed, most of it had been used for grazing generations of cattle. While cattle are grazers like bison, they prefer different kinds of grasses than

bison do, and they tend to stay longer in one area than bison do. These differences in behavior result in a different ecological effect. The cattle had reduced diversity. Fire had also been discouraged, allowing woodlands to creep into the edges of the prairie.

The Nature Conservancy is bringing back the two major shapers of the tallgrass, bison and fire. In this way, they hope that the preserve will gradually become closer to what it once was.

People are working to bring back the tallgrass prairie in other places, too. Grand Prairie Friends of Illinois maintains eleven prairie preserves that are open to the public. Neal Smith National Wildlife Refuge, in central Iowa, has a goal of restoring 8,000 acres (about 3,000 hectares) of the original tallgrass prairie and oak savanna that existed before the area was settled in the 1840s. Seeds of native plants are being collected and planted. Fire and bison are being reintroduced.

Fortunately, many areas containing prairie potholes are preserved as part of the National Wildlife Refuge System. This government program was started in 1903 to provide homes for wildlife. In 1934 the Duck Stamp Law came into effect. Waterfowl hunters have to buy a special duck stamp every time they buy their hunting licenses. The money that is collected is used to buy and protect the wetlands where waterfowl breed. Most hunters gladly pay the fee, for it helps ensure that the birds will have places to breed and to stop to feed during their spring and fall migrations. National Wildlife Refuges are scattered all along the Mississippi Flyway.

Like any other ecosystem, the tallgrass prairie has evolved over thousands of years. The lives of countless plants, animals, and other organisms interact and connect in many ways to produce this beautiful environment. While all species have their role, some, such as big bluestem grass and the American bison, are especially important to the balance of the tallgrass prairie ecosystem. Fortunately, people now understand the importance of the tallgrass prairie ecosystem to the health of nature in North America and are trying to preserve and re-create some of this magnificent terrain.

WE CAN ALL HELP PRESERVE AND RESTORE THE TALLGRASS PRAIRIE.

WHAT YOU CAN DO

PROTECTING GRASSLAND ECOSYSTEMS

The American prairies used to blanket the middle third of North America, but they aren't the only grasslands on the continent. There are desert grasslands, intermountain grasslands, California grasslands, and eastern grasslands as well. Wherever you live, there's a good chance that some kind of grassland is nearby, and there are ways you can help bring back and preserve our grasslands. Here are some suggestions:

• If you have a yard, talk to your parents about returning some of the lawn to a natural unmowed and unwatered state. Not only will you bring back wild grassland, you will also save on water and save on energy as well as reduce pollution by reducing mowing. In many areas, you can buy seeds for native grasses and wildflowers. Be sure to check local regulations, since mowed lawns are required in some areas.

• Find out what wildlife refuges, parks, and preserves with grasslands exist in your area. If you belong to a scout troup or other youth club, organize your group to volunteer—preserves always can use people to help pull out nonnative plants and perform other chores.

• Learn more about grasslands and give an oral report in your classroom about the subject so your fellow students can come to appreciate this special type of ecosystem.

• Get involved if proposals come up in your area to turn grasslands into housing developments, malls, or other forms of development.

WHAT HAPPENS IN THE FUTURE? YOU CAN BE INVOLVED

Find out if there is a grassland restoration project in your area and get involved. Keep up on proposals at the national level that will affect our grasslands, and write to the president and your congressional representatives. Here are some addresses you can use.

To write to the president:
The President
The White House
Washington, DC 20500

To write to the senators from your state:
The Honorable (name of your senator)
United States Senate
Washington, DC 20510

To write to your representative in Congress:
The Honorable (name of your representative)
U.S. House of Representatives
Washington, DC 20515

WEBSITES TO VISIT FOR MORE INFORMATION

There are many websites with more information about the tallgrass prairie in the United States and Canada. Here are a few of the most useful ones:

Iowa Prairie Network
<www.iowaprairienetwork.org>
The Iowa Prairie Network website provides answers to frequently asked questions about prairies, information on tallgrass locations in Iowa, and a list of interesting links.

Konza Prairie Long Term Ecological Research Program
<climate.konza.ksu.edu>
The Konza Prairie Long Term Ecological Research Program site provides information about Konza Prairie and the research carried on there. It also has an image gallery that's free for educational uses such as posters and reports.

Northern Prairie Wildlife Research Center

<www.npwrc.usgs.gov>

The Northern Prairie Wildlife Research Center, located in North Dakota, is operated by the U.S. Geological Survey and works to support sound management and conservation of prairies. On their website, you can find lots of information and can send a prairie postcard to a friend.

Prairies Forever

<www.prairies.org>

Prairies Forever gives information on creating a prairie garden, tips on getting involved, and lots of links.

Prairie Frontier

<www.prairiefrontier.com>

The Prairie Frontier sells wild grass and wildflower seeds, and the website features photos of many prairie plants and animals.

University of Minnesota Prairie Site

<www1.umn.edu/bellmuse/mnideals/prairie>

The University of Minnesota prairie site provides an interactive prairie restoration game, answers to questions about the prairie, and QuickTime clips. The curriculum page provides a list of prairie preserves around the United States, a list of links, and a pronunciation guide to Dakota Indian prairie terms such as names for prairie plants and animals.

FOR FURTHER READING

Johnson, Rebecca L. *A Walk in the Prairie.* Minneapolis: Carolrhoda Books, 2001.

Madson, John. *Tallgrass Prairie.* Helena, MT: Falcon Press, 1993.

———. *Where the Sky Began: Land of the Tallgrass Prairie.* Ames, IA: Iowa State University Press, 1995.

McClung, Robert M. *Lost Wild America: The Story of Our Extinct and Vanishing Wildlife.* Hamden, CT: Linnet Books, 1993.

Patent, Dorothy Hinshaw. *Biodiversity.* New York: Clarion Books, 1996.

Scott, Michael. *Ecology.* New York: Oxford University Press, 1995.

Shirley, Shirley. *Restoring the Tallgrass Prairie: An Illustrated Manual for Iowa and the Upper Midwest.* Iowa City: University of Iowa Press, 1994.

Smith, Annick. *Big Bluestem: Journey into the Tall Grass.* Tulsa, OK: Council Oaks Books, 1996.

VanCleave, Janice. *Ecology for Every Kid: Easy Activities that Make Learning About Science Fun.* New York: John Wiley & Sons, 1996.

Whitman, Sylvia. *This Land Is Your Land: The American Conservation Movement.* Minneapolis: Lerner Publications Company, 1994.

GLOSSARY

annual: a plant that lives for only one year

biodiversity: the variety of living things in an ecosystem

biomass: the total amount of plant and animal material in a given place

biennial: a plant that lives for two years

carbohydrates: a class of chemicals that includes sugars and starches

chlorophyll: the green chemical in plants that traps the energy of the sun

decomposer: a living thing that breaks down dead plants and animals into simple nutrients that can be used again by plants

ecosystem: a particular community of living things interacting with each other and their nonliving environment

edge effect: the increase in biodiversity at the boundary between two different types of habitats

forbs: leafy, nonwoody plants that are not grasses

legumes: members of the pea family

mixed prairie: the prairie between the tallgrass and short-grass prairie where the grasses generally stand from 2 to 4 feet (about 1 meter) tall

perennial: a plant that lives for more than two years

photosynthesis: the process by which green plants capture energy from the sun and use it to combine carbon dioxide and water to make their own food

pollen: the male reproductive material of a flowering plant, usually yellow in color

pollinator: an animal such as a bee, butterfly, or hummingbird that transfers pollen from one flower to another

primary consumer: a living thing that eats plants

primary producer: a living thing, usually a green plant, that converts the energy of the sun into chemical energy

rhizome: an underground stem of a plant

secondary consumer: a living thing, usually an animal, that eats primary consumers or other secondary consumers. Secondary consumers are also called predators.

short-grass prairie: a prairie that is made up largely of grasses about 20 inches (50 centimeters) tall

sod: the thick tangled mat of plant roots, stolons, and rhizomes that holds the soil firmly together

stolon: a plant stem that runs along the surface of the soil and produces new shoots

tallgrass prairie: the easternmost type of prairie, where grasses typically reach 5 to 6 feet (nearly 2 meters) tall

INDEX

ABOUT THE AUTHOR

Dorothy Hinshaw Patent is the author of over one hundred nonfiction books for children, including *Dogs: The Wolf Within, Polar Bears, Biodiversity,* and *Charles Darwin: The Life of a Revolutionary Thinker.* She has a Ph.D. in zoology from the University of California. She has two grown sons and a grandson and granddaughter. She lives in Missoula, Montana, with her husband, Greg.

ABOUT THE PHOTOGRAPHER

William Muñoz has worked as a nature photographer for over twenty years. You can see his photos of animals and plants in many books for children, including *Dogs: The Wolf Within, Horses,* and *Waiting Alligators.* He lives on Vancouver Island in British Columbia, Canada, with his wife and son.

PHOTO ACKNOWLEDGMENTS

All photographs © William Muñoz, except: © Tom Bean, p. 14; © Greg Neise/Visuals Unlimited, p. 26 (left); © Bill Johnson/Visuals Unlimited, p. 27 (left); © Robert Calentine/Visuals Unlimited, p. 37 (left); © Science VU/Visuals Unlimited, p. 37 (right); © Arthur M. Siegelman/Visuals Unlimited, p. 40 (right); © Joe McDonald/Visuals Unlimited, p. 47; © Richard Thom/Visuals Unlimited, p. 63. Maps and illustrations on pp. 9, 25, 38, and 54 by Tim Seeley.